Alaska Seafood
COOKBOOK

Salmon Spawning, Photo © 2008 Malthias Breiter/AccentAlaska.com

© Distributed by Arctic Circle Enterprises, LLC
3812 Spenard Rd. #100
Anchorage, Alaska 99517

© 2008 Designed and Published by Terrell Creative
P.O. Box 34260 • Kansas City, MO 64120
No part of this book may be reproduced without the consent of the publisher.
Designed in USA
Printed in China • 08C0115

Front Cover: Opilio Snow Crab Season on the Bering Sea, Photo © 2008 Josh Roper/AccentAlaska.com
Back Cover: Sitka Channel, the ANB Harbor and Sisters Mountain, Photo © 2008 Kim Heacox/AccentAlaska.com
Page 1: Salmon Fishing Fleets in the Kenai River, Photo © 2008 Greg Daniels/AccentAlaska.com

ISBN-13: 978-1-56944-378-1
ISBN-10: 1-56944-378-5

Recipes, Food Preparation and Food Presentation by Carol Luman
Food Photography by Chad Combs © Terrell Creative
Food Styling by Dean Eichler

Alaskan Seafood

Kodiak Island Harbor, Photo © 2008 Tony Lara/AccentAlaska.com

Alaskan King Crab

King Crab Cannelloni {WITH PINK BÉCHAMEL SAUCE}

Pasta:
- 2 cups semolina flour
- 2 large eggs
- 1 tsp. salt

- ~ *(or use 1 box cannelloni shells, about 10-12)*

Filling:
- 1 cup ricotta cheese
- ½ cup grated Parmesan cheese
- 1 egg yolk
- ¼ cup fresh basil, chopped
- 1½ lbs. king crab meat
- ~ salt and pepper to taste

Pasta:

In a food processor, add eggs, and with machine running, add dry ingredients. Process for about 1 minute, until coarse crumbs form. If mixture is too dry add 1 Tbsp. of water while machine is running. Form into a ball and wrap in plastic until ready to roll into sheets using your pasta machine. Follow your pasta machine's directions when rolling out your pasta. Cut each pasta sheet into 6x9–inch pieces.

Filling:

In a large bowl, combine ricotta, cheese, egg yolk, basil and salt and pepper. Gently fold in king crab meat. Place 3 Tbsp. of filling along width of pasta sheet, roll up and place seam side down in greased baking dish. *Or if using boxed pasta shells: Cook dry pasta until tender but firm to the bite, drain well.* Fill each shell and place in greased baking dish. Pour béchamel sauce over filled cannelloni and bake in 350°F. oven for 20 minutes, until bubbly. *(Pink Béchamel Sauce on following page)*

Pink Béchamel Sauce:

6	Tbsp. butter	2	Tbsp. tomato paste
2	cloves garlic, minced	½	tsp. salt
6	Tbsp. all-purpose flour	~	Pinch of nutmeg, freshly grated
4	cups whole milk, warmed	~	Pinch of white pepper

In a medium saucepan, melt butter over medium heat and sauté garlic for 2 minutes. Add flour and whisk for about 2 minutes, careful to not to let it brown. Gradually whisk in warm milk and tomato paste, continuing to whisk for 8-10 minutes or until sauce is thick and creamy. Remove from heat and whisk in salt, nutmeg and pepper.

Crab and Prawn Nachos

2	Tbsp. butter	½	tsp. ground cumin
½	lb. spot prawns, shelled, deveined, and chopped	3	cups Chihuahua or Jack cheese, grated
½	lb. steamed crab meat	~	pickled jalapeño slices for garnish
1	8 oz. sour cream	~	sturdy tortilla chips

Melt butter in saucepan; add chopped prawns and sauté until barely pink. Remove from heat and let cool. Stir in crab meat, sour cream and cumin. Season with salt and pepper to taste. Place 1 Tbsp. of mixture on tortillas and cover with grated cheese. Place nachos on a large baking sheet and broil until cheese is melted. Top each with jalapeño slice and serve.

Dutch Harbor Fishing Docks, Photo © 2008 Daryl Kyra Lee/AccentAlaska.com

King Crab Bisque

1½	cups sweet onion, finely chopped		3	cups king crab or fish stock
½	cup carrots, finely chopped		1½	cups heavy cream, room temperature
½	cup celery, finely chopped		2	tsp. salt
½	cup olive oil		1	tsp. cayenne pepper
1	Tbsp. fresh thyme, minced		1	lb. king crab meat
3	Tbsp. garlic, minced		¼	cup chives, minced
½	cup all-purpose flour		4-6	king crab legs, steamed

In large soup pot, heat oil over medium heat. Add onion, carrot and celery, sauté for 5 minutes until tender. Add thyme and garlic, stirring for about 1 minute. Sprinkle flour over sautéed vegetables. Using a wooden spoon, stir to coat evenly. Continue to stir for about 2-3 minutes, until a thick roux forms. Whisk in stock, stirring until blended. Bring to a gentle boil. Reduce heat; simmer uncovered, stirring often for about 30 minutes. Pour soup into blender and purée until smooth. Add cream, salt, cayenne pepper and crab meat. Simmer to warm crab meat. Adjust seasonings to taste. Serve in warm soup bowls. Garnish with chives and crab leg.

Open-Face King Crab Rangoon

2	8 oz. packages cream cheese, softened
2	tsp. garlic, minced
1	tsp. lemon juice
1	tsp. soy sauce
1	tsp. Worcestershire sauce
1	cup heavy cream

1	lb. king crab meat
1	cup green onion, chopped
¼	cup chives, minced
1	package egg roll wrappers
~	peanut oil for frying

In medium saucepan, combine cream cheese, garlic, lemon juice, soy and Worcestershire sauces over medium heat. Add cream a little at a time to desired thickness. Gently simmer for 5 minutes. Fold in crab meat and ½ cup green onion and remove from heat.

Heat 2 inches of peanut oil in deep skillet to 350°F. Fry egg roll wrappers until golden brown and drain on paper towels. Immediately dust with minced chives and salt to taste.

Spoon crab mixture on one wrapper, sprinkle with additional green onion.
Top with another egg roll wrapper.

Dipping Sauces {FOR STEAMED KING CRAB}

Cucumber–Yogurt Sauce
- 1 cup cucumber, seeded and drained
- 1 cup plain yogurt
- ¼ cup mayonnaise
- 1 Tbsp. grated onion
- 1 Tbsp. green onion, chopped
- 1 Tbsp. fresh lemon juice
- 1 tsp. spicy mustard
- ~ salt and pepper to taste

Combine all ingredients, mixing well. Chill.

Hot and Spicy Butter Sauce
- 2 sticks salted butter, melted
- 2 tsp. Worcestershire sauce
- 3 tsp. spicy grained mustard
- 2 Tbsp. chili sauce
- 1 Tbsp. fresh lemon juice
- 1 Tbsp. fresh chive, finely chopped
- 4-5 drops of hot pepper sauce
- ~ pinch of cayenne pepper

Heat all ingredients over medium heat to blend flavors. Serve warm.

Herb Butter Sauce
- 2 sticks unsalted butter
- 1 Tbsp. finely chopped of each: dill, tarragon, chive parsley
- 1 tsp. finely minced garlic
- ~ juice and zest of 1 lemon
- ~ salt and pepper to taste

Heat all ingredients over medium heat to blend flavors. Serve warm.

Alaskan Salmon

Salmon Seining in Sitka, Photo © 2008 Ken Graham/AccentAlaska.com

Braised Salmon

4	8 oz. silver king salmon fillets		3	cups red new potatoes, sliced
2	Tbsp. olive oil		2	cups plum tomatoes, diced
			1	Tbsp. tomato paste
¾	cup carrots, sliced		1	quart shrimp stock
¾	cup celery, sliced			
¾	cup fennel, sliced		~	Fennel tops for garnish
¾	cup sweet onion, sliced		~	salt and pepper to taste

Rinse salmon fillets and dry with paper towels; season both sides with salt and pepper. Heat oil in large ovenproof skillet. Add salmon, flesh side down and sear on both sides until golden brown. Remove from pan and set aside.

Add carrots, celery, fennel, and onion; sauté until soft. Add tomato paste and stock; stir well to combine. Add potatoes and tomatoes and sprinkle with fresh herbs. Place salmon fillets in pan on top of vegetables. Cover and place in 375°F. oven for 15 minutes or until potatoes are tender and fish is cooked through.

Using slotted spoon, carefully remove salmon and set aside. Ladle vegetable mixture into serving bowls and top with salmon and a sprig of fennel for garnish.

Potlatch Salmon

1 whole salmon	3 tsp. dry mustard
6 Tbsp. butter, softened	¾ cup brown sugar
~ juice of 1 lemon	~ heavy-duty foil

Butterfly salmon, remove head, tail and fins. Run knife down backbone of fish until it opens flat, careful not to cut through. You can also have your fish monger or meat manager prepare this for you. Tear off a sheet of heavy-duty foil large enough to handle the salmon; coat lightly with cooking spray. Place salmon skin-side down on foil. Spread softened butter over flesh of fish, drizzle with lemon juice and dry mustard. Cover with brown sugar, using more sugar if needed. Place foil with fish on barbeque grill over low heat; cover. Bake for 20 to 30 minutes. Salmon is cooked when flesh flakes easily.

Salmon fisherman line the banks at the confluence of the Russian and Kenai Rivers, casting into the sockeye salmon-filled water hoping to bring in a catch.
Photo © 2008 Ken Grahan/AccentAlaska.com

Planked King Salmon {WITH BLACKBERRY BUTTER SAUCE}

2	1-inch-thick cedar boards, large enough to hold fillets
6	8 oz. king salmon steaks
½	cup melted butter
~	juice of one lemon
1	tsp. fresh thyme
~	salt and pepper to taste

Blackberry Butter Sauce:

2	Tbsp. shallots, minced
1	clove garlic, minced
¼	cup balsamic vinegar
1	cup fresh blackberries
¼	cup white wine

Soak cedar in water for at least 1 hour before using.

Place 3 steaks on each cedar plank, brush with melted butter. Squeeze lemon over the fillets, season with salt and pepper. Place planks in a 350°F. oven and bake for 7-8 minutes or until firm. Remove fish with wide spatula to serving plate; top with sauce.

Blackberry Butter Sauce:
Place shallot, garlic, vinegar and berries in saucepan. Over high heat, reduce to about 1 Tbsp. Add wine and reduce again to about 1 Tbsp. of liquid. Lower heat and whisk in butter a few pieces at a time, melting each piece before adding more. Strain mixture into small bowl. Keep warm until ready to use (insulated pitcher or thermos works well).

Smoked Salmon-Wrapped Asparagus

Grapefruit Vinaigrette Marinade:
- 1 whole egg
- ½ cup fresh basil leaves
- 3 cloves garlic, crushed
- 1 tsp. fresh ground pepper
- 1 tsp. salt
- 3 Tbsp. red wine vinegar

- 1½ cup vegetable oil
- ¾ cup fresh grapefruit juice

Asparagus:
- 1 lb. fresh asparagus, trimmed
- ~ sliced smoked salmon, approximately 12–14 slices

Grapefruit Vinaigrette Marinade:
In a food processor or blender, combine egg, basil, garlic, pepper, salt and vinegar. Process about 30 seconds. Slowly add oil in a stream to make a mayonnaise. Thin this mixture with grapefruit juice to desired consistency.

Asparagus:
Steam asparagus over boiling water for 3-5 minutes. Place in ice bath immediately; pat dry and place in plastic bag. Add vinaigrette and marinate for 1 hour. Drain asparagus and wrap each in 1 slice of salmon. Serve as an appetizer or side dish.

Fish Stock

5	lbs. white fish bones, tails and heads	2	bay leaves
2	medium onions, coarsely chopped	15	peppercorns
3	celery stalks, coarsely chopped	6	sprigs parsley
3	carrots, coarsely chopped	2	cups white wine
2	tsp. dried thyme		

Rinse fish bones under cold running water, making sure the gills have been removed. Place vegetables and remaining ingredients in large stockpot. Add fish bones and enough cold water to cover. Bring to a boil and reduce to low heat. Simmer, skimming the foam as it rises, for 30 minutes. Line a strainer with a dampened cheesecloth or tea towel and place over clean pot. Let stock cool completely. Pour stock into quart containers and a few ice cube trays. Refrigerate for up to 2 days or freeze indefinitely.

Spawning Red Salmon, Photo © 2008 Natalie Fobes/AccentAlaska.com

Smoked Salmon Frittata

6	large eggs		2	Tbsp. cream cheese, cut in cubes and softened
2	Tbsp. milk			
1	Tbsp. fresh dill, minced		3	oz. smoked salmon, chopped
¼	tsp. freshly grated nutmeg		3	tsp. olive oil
2	Tbsp. fresh chives, minced		~	salt and pepper to taste

Whisk eggs, milk, dill, nutmeg, salt, pepper and chives together in large bowl. Fold the cream cheese and salmon into egg mixture. Heat oil in a 10″ skillet over medium-high heat. Add egg mixture to skillet and stir gently to distribute fillings. Cook eggs until bottom is set but not browned, about 3 minutes. Transfer skillet to center rack in a 350°F. oven and bake until top is set, about 8 minutes. Can add additional salmon to top if desired at about 4 minutes. Remove from oven and let set for about 5 minutes. Cut into wedges or invert onto serving platter.

Court-Bouillon {FOR POACHING FISH}

1	carrot, sliced	1	tsp. white peppercorns
1	small stalk celery, sliced	2	sprigs of flat leaf parsley
½	small onion, sliced	1	cup white wine
1	bay leaf	2	quarts water

Mix all ingredients in a stainless steel or enamel saucepan. Bring to a boil, reduce heat, and simmer 10 minutes. Cool and strain. Add cooled court-bouillon to poaching pan; add fish and increase heat gradually, especially with whole or large pieces. Poach until fish flakes easily.

Salmon Fishing in Anchorage, Photo © 2008 Ken Graham/AccentAlaska.com

Halibut Fishing in Cook Inlet, Photo © 2008 Greg Daniels/AccentAlaska.com

Halibut Packets

4	8 oz. halibut fillets
~	paprika
~	salt
~	fresh ground pepper
4	tsp. fresh rosemary, chopped
2	small onions, thinly sliced
8	large black olives, quartered
½	red bell pepper, thinly sliced
~	juice of 1 lemon
8	Tbsp. olive oil or melted butter
~	parchment paper

Cut 4 parchment paper hearts 12″ long and 12″ wide. Oil hearts well. Place fillets on oiled hearts. Season fillets with salt, ground pepper and a liberal sprinkling of paprika. Sprinkle ½ tsp. of rosemary on each fillet and top with pepper, onion and olives. Drizzle lemon juice evenly over each fillet, then 2 Tbsp. of olive oil. Seal edges of hearts by folding up edges and pinching closed. It's helpful to start at the top of the heart shape and end at bottom, tucking the point of paper underneath packet. Grill over hot coals for about 10 minutes. Cooking time will vary with thickness of fillet. Transfer packets to warm plates; open with sharp knife when ready to serve.

Cocktail Sauce

3	cups ketchup		1	tsp. kosher salt
⅓	cup onion, minced		1	tsp. fresh ground pepper
⅓	cup celery, minced		~	juice of 1 lemon
1	Tbsp. horseradish		~	hot sauce to taste

Mix all ingredients well; chill well before serving.

Tartar Sauce

2	cups mayonnaise		½	cup dill pickle relish
¾	tsp. hot mustard		1	cup sweet onion, sliced
¼	tsp. fresh ground pepper		½	cup flat leaf parsley
¼	tsp. kosher salt		2	Tbsp. capers

Combine mayonnaise, mustard, pepper, salt and relish. Using a blender, grind onion, parsley and capers. Add to mayonnaise and mix well.

A boat passes inside Entrance Island, Valdez Narrows, Prince William Sound.
Photo © 2008 Ron Niebrugge/AccentAlaska.com

Steamed Halibut {WITH MANGO SAUCE}

Halibut:
- 1 lemon, cut into wedges
- 1 Tbsp. fresh ginger, sliced
- 2-3 leek leaves
- 6 8 oz. halibut fillets

Mango Sauce:
- 1 cup fresh orange juice
- ½ cup fresh lemon juice
- ¼ cup chili sauce

- 1 cup frozen mango, chopped and defrosted
- 1 cup sugar
- ½ cup white vinegar
- 1 tsp. fresh ginger, chopped

Cornstarch Thickener:
- ½ cup cornstarch
- 4 Tbsp. cold water

Halibut:

Place water, lemon and ginger in bottom of steamer. Bring to a boil with lid on. Place leek leaves on bottom of steamer, add fillets and place steamer tray over boiling water. Steam for 10 minutes or until halibut is firm to the touch. Serve on warm plates with mango sauce.

Mango Sauce:

Bring all ingredients to a boil. Simmer for 5 minutes. Slowly add cornstarch mixture through straining sieve a little at a time to thicken.

Cornstarch Thickener:

Add cold water to cornstarch 1 Tbsp. at a time until well blended.

Halibut Tacos {WITH PEPPER SLAW}

Batter:
- ¾ cup all-purpose flour
- ¾ cup cornstarch
- ½ tsp. baking soda
- 2 tsp. salt
- ¼ tsp. ground pepper
- ¼ tsp. garlic powder
- ¼ tsp. paprika
- ¼ tsp. dried dill
- ¼ tsp. dried thyme

- ½ tsp. lemon zest
- ½ cup dark beer
- ½ cup water

Halibut:
- 1½ lb. fresh halibut cut diagonally into 12 or more pieces
- ~ peanut oil for frying
- ~ flour for dusting
- ~ flour tortillas, warmed

Batter:
In a large bowl, combine all the dry ingredients. Stir in beer, water and lemon zest to make a light batter. Add 1-2 Tbsp. of water as needed.

Fish:
Heat 5-inch depth of oil in fryer or Dutch oven to 375°F. Dust a piece of fish in flour and then dip in batter. Carefully drop a few pieces at a time into the hot oil. Cook until golden brown, about 3 minutes. Drain well on paper sacks while frying remaining pieces. In warm tortilla, place spoonful of slaw *(Pepper Slaw recipe on opposite page)*, top with one or more pieces of fish and garnish with favorite hot sauce.

Pepper Slaw {FOR HALIBUT TACOS}

Pepper Slaw:

1	red bell pepper, cut into strips		1	bunch green onion, sliced
1	yellow bell pepper, cut into strips		¼	cup white wine vinegar
1	green pepper, cut into strips		3	Tbsp. vegetable oil
1	cup cabbage, sliced		2	Tbsp. sugar

Combine vegetables in large bowl. Place dressing ingredients in a jar with a lid and shake well to combine. Pour over slaw and chill for several hours.

Halibut Catch
Photo © 2008 Doug Wilson/AccentAlaska.com

Pan-Seared Halibut Steaks {WITH ROASTED ASPARAGUS}

Halibut:
- ½ cup olive oil
- 3 Tbsp. butter
- 4 6 oz. halibut steaks
- ~ flour for dusting
- ~ salt & pepper to taste

Asparagus:
- 1 lb. young asparagus, trimmed and cleaned
- 2 small shallots, minced
- 3 cloves garlic, minced
- 4 Tbsp. olive oil

Halibut:
Rinse halibut and pat dry. Season with salt and pepper and dust lightly with flour, shaking off excess. Heat oil and butter in small saucepan. Heat grill pan over medium-high heat; brush with butter and oil mixture. Add steaks and brown 3-4 minutes on each side. Brush with more butter/oil mixture if needed, before turning.

Asparagus:
In large bowl combine seasonings and whisk to blend. Add asparagus and toss to coat. Season with salt and pepper to taste. Using tongs place asparagus on grill pan and roast for 10 minutes or until tender.

Place 4-5 asparagus spears on serving plate, top with fillet and garnish with a drizzle of olive oil.

Shellfish Stock

2 ½	lbs. shrimp or crab shells
2 ½	quarts cold water
1	cup onion, coarsely chopped
½	cup carrots, chopped
½	cup celery, chopped

1	Tbsp. garlic, coarsely chopped
~	make a sachet of:
	1 bay leaf, ½ tsp. dried thyme,
	½ tsp. black peppercorn and
	6 flat parsley stems

Rinse shells under cold water and place in large stockpot along with the remaining ingredients. Bring to a boil and lower temperature and simmer for 45 minutes to 1 hour. Skim foam as it rises. Strain stock and cool immediately using an ice bath. Refrigerate for up to 2 days or freeze.

Cleaning Oyster Lanterns, Peterson Bay, Photo © 2008 Glenn Oliver/AccentAlaska.com

Shellfish

Aerial of Simpson Bay, Eastern Prince William Sound,
Photo © 2008 Ron Niebrugge/AccentAlaska.com

Kodiak Scallops {WITH SAUTÉED PEPPERS AND POLENTA}

Scallops:
- 2 lbs. Kodiak scallops
- ¼ cup olive oil
- 1 each, red, yellow and orange pepper, sliced in strips

Polenta:
- 1 cup seafood stock
- 7 cups water
- 2 Tbsp. olive oil
- 2 Tbsp. unsalted butter
- 2 cups polenta *(coarsely ground cornmeal)*
- 1 cup fresh Parmesan cheese, grated
- 1 tsp. salt
- ~ pepper to taste

Scallops:

Toss scallops in olive oil. Heat large nonstick skillet over medium-high heat; drain the olive oil from scallops into skillet. Add scallops in a single layer and sauté 2-3 minutes or until they are golden brown. Carefully turn the scallops and brown on other side for 1-2 minutes; remove scallops. Add peppers to pan and cook 2-3 minutes before turning, cooking until tender but still crunchy.

Polenta:

Bring the water and stock to a boil in a large saucepan; add oil, butter and salt. Reduce heat to low. Slowly whisk in the polenta, stirring constantly for 15–20 minutes or until mixture is small and thickened. Stir in cheese and season with pepper. Cover and remove from heat; keep warm until ready to serve.

Photo © 2008 Glenn Oliver/
AccentAlaska.com

Tempura Spot Prawn {WITH LETTUCE CUPS AND SEAFOOD FRIED RICE}

12   spot prawns, peeled and deveined
~   peanut oil for deep-frying

Tempura Batter:

1   egg
1   cup ice water
½   tsp. salt

1   cup all-purpose flour plus
½   cup for dusting
1½   tsp. baking powder

Prepare batter when ready to begin frying. Beat egg and ice water together until combined. Combine flour, baking powder and salt. Add dry ingredients to egg mixture and stir lightly until just blended. Rinse and pat dry prawns. Dip prawns in additional flour and shake off excess. Using a fork or skewer, dip prawns one at a time into batter, letting excess drain back into bowl. Fry prawns in 350°F. oil for 2-3 minutes each. Drain on paper towels and keep warm until ready to serve.

(Lettuce Cups and Seafood Fried Rice Recipes on Following Page)

Spot Prawn, Photo © 2008 Pat Costello/
AccentAlaska.com

Seafood Fried Rice:

¼	cup vegetable oil
½	cup fresh crab meat
½	cup scallops, finely diced
¼	cup carrots, finely diced
1	small onion, finely diced
2	eggs, beaten
3½	cups cooked long-grain rice prepared the day before
1	bunch bean sprouts
1	tsp. soy sauce
1	bunch green onions, sliced
~	salt and pepper to taste

Lettuce Cups:

2	heads Boston Bibb lettuce *(rinsed and separated into individual cups)*

Garnish suggestions:

~	Chopped peanuts and cashews, sliced green onions, pickled Chinese vegetables, favorite Asian sauces

Heat wok or heavy skillet over high heat until hot. Add ½ of the oil and heat for 30 seconds. Add seafood, carrots and onion; stir-fry for 3 minutes. Remove seafood and vegetables with slotted spoon. Discard oil. Add remaining oil and heat 30 seconds. Add beaten eggs, and let set for a couple of seconds. Reduce heat to medium-high; add rice and toss to combine with egg. Add seafood, sautéed vegetables, sprouts and soy sauce; toss until heated through. Season with salt and pepper and garnish with green onions. Place seafood rice carefully into the lettuce cups that you have prepared. Lay the Tempura Spot Prawn on top, and finish off with your favorite garnish.

Digging for Razor Clams, Mt. Redoubt. Photo © 2008 Glen Oliver/AccentAlaska.com

Seafood Pot Pie

½	cup butter	3	cups seafood stock or seafood bouillon
½	cup all-purpose flour	1	tsp. hot sauce
1	tsp. salt	2	cups potatoes, cubed
½	cup onion, finely chopped	1	cup carrots, cubed
¼	cup fennel, finely chopped	1	cup frozen peas
½	cup chopped celery	12	spot prawns, chopped
2	cloves garlic, minced	1	lb. crab meat
1	cup whole milk		

Melt butter in large saucepan over medium heat. Sauté onion, fennel, garlic and celery for 3 minutes. Blend in flour and salt; cook for 3 minutes. Gradually stir in stock. Cook, stirring constantly until smooth and thickened; simmer for 8–10 minutes. Stir in milk and hot sauce; continue to cook for 5 minutes. Remove from heat. In a small saucepan, cover potatoes and carrots with water and simmer for 5 minutes; drain. Add potatoes, carrots, peas and seafood to sauce. Mix well and pour into a buttered casserole dish or individual ramekins. Top with crust and bake in 425°F. oven until golden brown.

Salmon Fishing, Southeast Alaska, Photo © 2008 Guy Hoppen/AccentAlaska.com